A Strange Arrangement

DP&

A Strange Arrangement

New & Selected Poems

C. J. Allen

- Leafe Press -

Published by Leafe Press,
4 Cohen Close
Chilwell
Nottingham
NG9 6RW
United Kingdom

www.leafepress.com

A catalogue record for this book is available from the British Library

ISBN: 0-9535401-5-4

Cover photograph 'This Danish Summer' by Jean Schweitzer. Used
with permission. Copyright © Jean Schweitzer. All right reserved.

Acknowledgements

Acknowledgements are due to the editors of the following publications/websites where some of the poems first appeared:

Iota, Ver Poets Anthologies 2004 & 2005, The Coffee House, Lancaster Litfest Anthologies 2000, 2003 & 2005, Brando's Hat, Staple, Other Poetry, Miracle & Clockwork (Other Poetry Press 2005), Poetry Nottingham, Paging Doctor Jazz (Shoestring Press 2004), The Interpreter's House, (www)Exultations & Difficulties, (www)Litter, (www)Stride, Poetry: The Nottingham Collection (Five Leaves Press 2005), (www)ShadowTrain, The Rialto

'The Future Body' was written for the Retina Dance Company's production 'Eleven Stories for the Body' (2005), and first appeared in the programme for the show.

Thanks to A.B., A.B. & M.S. who have, over the years, been the very best of poetry friends.

Special thanks to Alan Baker, gentleman poetry publisher, for making it all happen.

Contents

A Strange Arrangement

in memory of Arthur Allen
1920 – 2005

Anthony Earnshaw and the World of Poetic Conspiracy

Rising and sinking gasometers heave
Imperceptible sighs among
The pullulating ruins of
Chapeltown. A heavy rain
Falls like applause on the deaf streets
Where Anthony Earnshaw is collecting
186 lost combs.
Toothless and mutilated, they
Fill the gutters like leaves in autumn.

The evening sky is methylated,
The colour of wood spirit.
The shapes of the houses harden against it,
Becoming more and more real.

The collection of combs is almost complete.

The Water Turned to Blood
Early on in his career J. M. W. Turner planned to paint a subject
from the Apocalypse, titled 'The Water Turned to Blood'

Where web-footed gulls squat on the mud,
A man sits watching bridges hoop the Thames.
He wants to paint 'The Water Turned to Blood.'
The river chatters at his feet and gleams.

He grew up in a steamy barber's shop,
Swilling out the whiskered, foamy bowls
for his father, fetching him the soap,
the strap, the towels and the polished steels.

Now, he whips soft peaks of coloured oils
Onto a palette-knife and scrapes the blade
over a taut canvass; sail-cloth veils
absorb filaments of light and shade.

He paints the last days of a dying race,
Something being buried out at sea.
A tall ship is towed to its resting place,
Obsolete, into the nineteenth century.

Machinery has begun to flower
All about him, like the spindly weed
That chokes the oak. He watches light devour
The water, then glitteringly recede.

Soon, a heavy sky above the buildings
On the far bank smudges rooftops, turns
Treasure-houses of the late sun's gildings
Back to lead. Shadows shawl the cranes.

He paints his fascination with the point
Where sky and water meet and where men fuse
Into the elemental; the vague joint
Of heaven and earth. He paints a bruise

Of aquamarine and yellow-ochre,
As, river-chilled, night hangs in Hammersmith.
He stirs the hissing coals with a brass poker –
Black clinker with dimming pinks beneath –

And recalls the shining beads of blood
Clouding white enamel bowls, almost
Like skies from which the sun has disappeared,
Or a paintbrush giving up its watery ghost.

Guidelines for a Love Lyric

Start with a shadow.

Your poems needs to dwell
On ecstasies. If
You have none, write

Passionately about
Domestic circumstances.
Whispers and screams

Are, each in their own way,
Essential and ought
To be in there

Somewhere. Speak firmly
But not without tenderness –
Even if you have

To fake either
Or both. Be aware
Of the weather

But do not seek to draw
Comparisons between it
And your true love's

Anything. Say too much
If you must, or
Too little; never

Just enough. It looks
Calculating
And won't add up.

For maximum effect
Include revealing
Detail sparingly.

The contents of
Your fridge, for example,
Can often be devastating.

from *The Education Act*

This picture shows a black man with a spear
In South America; this is a map
Of who grows wheat and where; the very top
Of Everest (with Union Jack) is here

On the last page of the book. The sand
Of the Qatara is described in chapter
Nine; the drawing of the helicopter
Landing on what looks like a bandstand

In the ocean is an oil rig, vital
To our economy; the population
Growth in Third-World nations, an explosion
Of hungry faces underneath the title:

People of Many Lands. Do not scream.
These are only facts. Remember them.

Woodwork didn't work for me. It broke
Nobody's heart, however, that I couldn't
Chisel, plane or saw, or that I didn't
Make the bookends; it was a kind of joke.

And so when they said, 'Do Latin instead.'
I was relieved to butcher no more trees,
To close the tool-box lid on miseries
Endured for too many years. I read

The younger Pliny's polished correspondence
While others, ankle-deep in scrolls of grain,
Fashioned epic furniture from the plain
Facts of timber. Growling blades cut dense

Forests down to size and made them fit,
As Rome built up an empire and lost it.

'Write a poem,' she said. 'Keep it short;
Use plenty of adjectives; write about how
You feel a lot. War's a good subject, or Sport,
Or Animals of course, The Wind, The Snow ...

Don't worry about making it rhyme,
This is 1969 and life
Is too complex. Time
Is a favourite with poets, likewise Grief.

These are just ideas. Be ironic
If you like. Feel free to express
Yourself but refrain from histrionic
Disclosures of emotion. We'll discuss

Them all next week and I'll say which I think
Are best and read them out.' My mind went blank.

And it all came down to this: a clock,
A fountain-pen, and memories; all racing.
The focused sun; the bored official pacing
The hunched ranks; the slow, unfolding shock

Of ignorance or bad luck. Others,
Locked in their silent bubble of recollection
Are of no help; there is no protection
In numbers at the end. Fear gathers

The brain's pieces together into a fact;
Faith and determination do the rest.
All of us, like fools, giving our best
Performances in the education act.

For what? if there is nothing that is sure,
Why, when they say, 'Stop writing,' is there always   more.

Radar Love
for Ann

The pier theatre had just gone dark
And we were at the water's edge, at dusk,
Sympathising with the sea's insomnia.

Like bits of midnight that had broken loose,
Agile bats danced above our heads,
Enjoying the resonance of our affection.

Mosaic

This smile from Herculaneum
Is fixed, just like a photograph.
These fragments of linoleum,
These phrases from a paragraph

Long forgotten linger here
For us to puzzle at, for us
To reassemble. *Over there,*
By that wall, stood the chorus ...

But they are lost, invisible,
Time's jigsaw unmakes itself
As we labour at the impossible
Task of a world that wakes itself

Each day by shuffling atoms, shedding
Hair, becoming something else.
The moment careers forward, heading
Out of control. Long, slow gales

Of history scatter kingdoms like
Fistfuls of grain on the milling surface
Of the planet. So we make
Amends, or try to. Piece by piece

Our shattered ancestors take shape:
A raised eyebrow; a stag at bay;
A string of pearls; antique landscape
That shimmers in the photoplay

Of afternoons slipped out of sight
And mind. And on this Roman floor,
In coloured glass, someone who might
Be you stands by a yellow door.

The Pottery Lighthouse

There, in the cabinet, is the pottery lighthouse,
A sectionally constructed, four-inch, pottery lighthouse
Which, when de-constructed, becomes a condiment set:
Salt- and pepper-cellars and a mustard pot,
With 'A Present from Southport' written on the mustard pot.
As a child I used to play with this condiment set,

But I snapped the tiny spoon in the mustard pot,
The tiny, bone-white spoon in the mustard pot.
So I rotated the base of the pottery lighthouse
To hide the broken spoon, and I never heard a word about it,
Got clean-as-daylight away with it, never heard a word about it
Until one day, my mother brought up the matter of the lighthouse

In an otherwise casual conversation,
Twenty years on, in casual conversation,
Do you remember that condiment set,
The one you used to play with, the one in the cabinet
The one with the broken spoon, in the cabinet,
Shaped like a lighthouse? I remembered the set

Shaped like a lighthouse and ingeniously constructed
In three neat stages, a sectionally constructed
Condiment set with a tiny white spoon
That snapped like a wishbone under my thumb,
Twenty years ago, in pieces, under my thumb.
And I remembered the fragments of tiny white spoon

In the mustard pot as I reassembled the lighthouse,
Being careful to rotate the base of the lighthouse
In order to conceal any signs of damage.
Now I'm looking down the years that separate the three of us -
Mother, son and pottery lighthouse, the three of us –
And I'm trying to assess any signs of damage.

Trophy

I hold up the cup
More like a begging bowl.
Bandy-legged, starved
As Gandhi, I smile weakly.

My Clarks sandals are
So new you can almost
Hear the leather creaking,
The polished buckle jingling;

Nonetheless, I am elated,
And their vanilla crepe,
Thick as marzipan,
Keeps my feet off the ground.

Being only nine,
The Beatles' new LP
And the International Times
Don't mean much to me.

This is my status symbol,
This snap of me looking
Anaemic, gripping the handles
Of the silver cup.

Awarded for making progress
In learning to swim,
Each week the chalice passed
To another hopeful.

But, for that moment,
Of all the non-swimmers,
I was the one
Least likely to drown.

This Morning

I do not want to go to work.
I want to go to work instead
on the birdsong filtering-in
through the bathroom window.

Or possibly the clouds.
I want to compile the long taxonomy
of my feelings, to finally explain
the meaning of rainfall

on suburban gardens,
and say why light through beech leaves
is both sad and elevating
at the same time.

I want to prove beyond all doubt
that the radio-alarm has a mind
of its own, and that the darkness,
when it comes, is only darkness.

No Place Like It

No ice-fields, icebergs, growlers, no
iridescent blueness in
the sunlight, just the deep-freeze in
the local supermarket. No
vaulted, sculpted, soaring stone,
no God-shaped holes plugged by a mass
of miraculous masonry, just a spireless
church in a field of bones. No talking
trees, no water sprites, no elves,
no knights on quests, no moats or castles,
just a newsagent's and a public 'phone,
some swings, a bus-shelter, a bowling green.
No eggheads in togas strolling in the shade,
just a gaggle of girls bunking off school,
discussing the qualities of someone called Carl.
No sacred river, no fountainhead,
no pilgrims washing their feet in the water,
nursing hopes of an overnight cure,
just a rusty beck and the new Health Centre.
No singing sands, no foothills where
mountains shelve in to a shadowed plain,
just a shopping precinct. No signs or wonders
in the air, no polished plaques
on the birthplaces of poets, just numbers.

The Balloon Goes Up

A self-destructive insect
beats severely at
the vicarage window,

where a clergyman is struggling
with his sermon – relating the kidneys
to the spiritual cleansing

of Christian baptism.
Meanwhile, the fanatical
verger, Mr. Hopkins,

is on the lawn, inflating
a hot-air balloon
from which he plans to scatter

improving tracts over
the parish. From time
to time, the vicar's thread

is snapped by fiery
exhalations as
the air-ship takes shape.

Unlatching the casement,
he admits a dazed wasp,
like a syllable of doubt,

into his study, and
asks Mr. Hopkins,
earnestly, if he

must do this. By now
the verger cannot hear,
poised beneath a spike

of flame. The telephone
jangles in the hall.
It is the bishop

again. He wants to know
what in heaven's name
is going on. Outside,

the balloon goes up
like a jellyfish
towards the sunlight.

Falling Off A Log

Slam! The world comes up
to meet you, cunningly

shifting its axes. Only
seconds ago you were on top

of things and now you're side
by side. You can't believe it.

You think *Maybe I'll give it
a second or two then slide*

back upright. But when you try
you find somebody or

something has oiled the floor
inside your head. The sky

swims and swoons before
resuming its freakish plane.

Grounded you check for pain.
Your arm's a little sore,

there is a very slight
stiffness in your knee.

Nothing you should be
at all concerned about,

nothing too awry.
So you make a second pull

back to the vertical.
This time you're home and dry.

Reality comes back
on stream without a defect.

Smug as a new prefect,
you're straight on the attack:

It was just a minor blip,
a bug, a glitch, a snag.

You don't mean to brag,
but that kind of slip

doesn't happen twice
to someone with your sense

of poise and confidence.
But you can't trust your advice.

Somehow it seems the ground
is waiting, lying low,

unsettling. And so,
you stop. You look around,

feeling faintly queasy.
You don't know how it happened,

the air suddenly deepened.
You could do it again. It's easy.

Stuart

Even though you were smaller than me
I looked up to you.
A kind of teenage Pericles,

tales of your enigmatic brevity were legion.
'Life,' you once offered,
'is like a very tight parking space.'

And, speaking of Kath Smith,
'That girl can hold her breath
longer than anyone else I know.'

You had everything:
a Marilyn Monroe T-shirt,
a Hillman Imp.

You knew why *The Lovin' Spoonful*
were called *The Lovin' Spoonful*.

Claude Lorrain – Landscape with the Nymph Egeria Mourning over Numa

1.
The figures are tiny. This is probably the moment before Diana emerges from the trees to commemorate such devoted mourning by dissolving Egeria's tear-racked body into an everlasting spring. It might be good to know more, but we don't. Except that soft spots of light nudge at the foliage. Certainly it isn't a faithful account of anywhere in particular. What seems to have mattered to the artist were the Classical principles: tall, waving trees; some people walking into a lakeside temple; ancient buildings dwarfed by brooding woodland. A silvered plane of lucidity and harmony. It could be dawn or evening; we can't tell simply by looking.

2.
Forget what it was you first thought of. Find yourself following a river that winds into the distance where a boat with a blue canopy is drawn up to some steps, and a pine tree stands by a crumbling colonnade. It's summer in the Empire of the Imagination. As you look on, water apes the trees and acres or cloud-loaded sky, wood-blurred ruins moralise on the transience of earthly things, and for a moment it seems as though you can see a little way into their depth.

From The Norwegian

She wakes up.   [3:32 A.M.]
For a moment she is still
in Trondheim,

but then realizes
she is thinking
in English.   [3:34 A.M.]

She goes to the window.
It is starting to snow.
At first only *sludd*,

then bigger, drier flakes
of *tør grenet*.
She climbs back into bed.   [3:36 A.M.]

Memory sifts-in:
A weatherboard house
in the country;

the sky overwhelmed
by snow;
her sister's voice

asking 'What language   [3:39 A.M.]
do you feel in?'
Snow tumbling

out of darkness.
She is laughing
with her sister

who is asleep   [4:00 A.M.]
in Denmark.
Outside, the snow

continues to fall
in Norwegian.
She wakes up.   [4:32 A.M.]

                                        [4: 40 A.M.]

Untitled, 1980s/I Disembarked at Neasden
for Ann, again

The Jubilee Line doodling

its way into North London,
chattering past Xeroxed back gardens,
closing like a zip on an unfashionable jacket.

I disembarked at Neasden,
joke capital of the North Circular,
orbital metropolis of nowhere in particular.

By the offices of the British Shoe Corporation
I watched big clouds muscle-in,
back-lit, urban-Wagnerian.

Somewhere over the bumpy horizon
you waited for me in your flat above the barber's,
our lives packed tightly inside us

like Jacks-in-their-boxes.

Civilization, its Discontents

Somewhere in Indonesia, a tribe
is holding out against Christ,
the dollar, the bribe
of the assault rifle and the training shoe, and just

for the hell of it, maybe, is sticking to
the ancient ways - which forbid voting,
poisoning fish, using toothpaste, touching
the breasts of virgins or having anything to do

with the wheel. They are a plucky bunch
whose goggle-eyed, pocket-size gods'
exceptional genitalia

greatly disturbed the last French
missionary who visited. His words,
they said, smelled strangely of magnolia.

Middle English

Call her the flaxen Saxon,
the hiking Viking,
a friend from the North
reeling you in with a fine line

in vocabulary temptingly
unfamiliar, but close enough
to lodge itself like an incubating pupa
in your speech. Remember

when *small* meant 'narrow, slender',
when *tool* meant 'weapon'? No longer,
no longer. It was soon after the Conquest

you found yourself struggling
with a new orthography, speaking to her
on your knees, in Middle English.

From a Battlefield
(at the site of the battle of East Stoke, 1487)

Rain the colour of blades, falling on water,
the dull finish of old metal. Water
collecting in the heart of England,
a country like a wet suburban garden
full of broken crockery, fragments of bone.

Someone exercising a dog called Harry,
a dog from a long dynasty
of dogs called Harry, the *chink* of a loosened choke-chain,
the *clank* of blade on basinet.
Harry rooting in gutters, sniffing in ditches.

A vole skedaddles along a slippery bank.
Walking in England, quietly forgetting
ranks of men at arms, their fires at night,
what they had to eat,
the muddy meaning of fields

strewn with remnants of heraldry,
one afternoon, one rainy afternoon.
The usual battlefield topography, a wood,
an incline, an uneven plain. A car parked
by the roadside, a couple of people

reading a map, pointing, then changing their minds.
A crow flies over the landscape
where something once happened. This could be
the crux, the hub, the centre.
Somewhere in England.

Kenneth

Except for himself of course, Schubert lieder
were the love of his life. Only music
of *Wintereisse*'s cancelling
whiteness could muffle the flutters of panic.

He watched the air over Green Park turn milky
then walked home alone. The Barclays,
more Schubert, the mating-calls
of pigeons he'd shoo off the window ledges.

A Fire-Engine in the Middle of England

A dog is barking repeatedly
at something that no-one else can see.
It's midday, midsummer and punishing heat
has driven everyone from the street.

Sunlight is chiselling chips of flint
from the river where, lost in contentment,
a man stands up to his waist and wades
in the water like the Jack of Spades.

He remembers from somewhere somebody saying
*There's a fine line between fishing and standing
on the bank looking stupid*, and he smiles.
The river pushes and twists for miles

through open country, past fields and woodland
to find its way to the middle of England.
A single car comes up the lane,
you can hear the engine-note complain

and dip a semitone or three
as it stops at a red light, grudgingly.
In the back seat is an eight year old boy
being driven home to some out of the way

market town. The window is down
and he trails his hand in air that's sown
with spores of willow herb and drifting seeds.
As the shop-signs and road-signs slide by he reads

each one aloud. His peroration
is suddenly halted by the fire station,
its big doors open, the flat-faced engine
glaring at the world in blazing sun.

And it's like the angel in the Book of Revelation,
that cries out to the gobsmacked population
on the final day all that business
about *the supper of the Mighty One* or some such nonsense

we never thought could possibly be true.
But then the lights turn green and the car moves through
its sequence of gears, away into the haze
of the afternoon. The fisherman sways

and casts once more over the mirrored river.
The dog goes on barking. A tiny shiver
passes through the boy like a brilliancy
that no-one else in the world can see.

Bargain

Everyone was happy; even the statisticians.
It was a day that inspired faith in the quotidian,
a morning suffused with the idea of living nobly,
like those chiselled Roman profiles
they had us contemplate years ago.

A wind came and the grass bent,
flowers nodded, grateful for their Latin names.
On a bitumen roof unseen pools
reflected bleary patches of sky
where auguries of starlings flew.

Time seemed to pass and the world happened.
Advertisements for better bodies, muscles
with lovelier and more specific gravity,
appeared in the press. All the while
dust whispered its quiet aphorisms.

It was so offhand. 'Here,' said a workman,
'hand me that wrench.' Clouds
hung over sprawling malls.
Rivers heavy with silt teemed in swart sashays.
We make our bargain for moments like these.

Screened by distance, crawling traffic
stalled on a bridge, hovers there
like beads on a string, a floating signifier,
a strange arrangement of grace
overshot by a few fistfuls of light.

Launch

Up in the trees bush babies
cling, randomly. From time to time
one falls onto the forest floor
with a slight, sickening thud.

Leaf-cutter ants manhandle their outsize sails
down to the underground shore
where they launch them
on seas of fungus.

Barely breaking surface tension,
frogs blip out of the river.
Something drags its oily tail
along the slimy bank.

You've been there, I feel sure,
plashing your way to the delta,
agog at rotten crocodile-logs
floating beside your canoe.

Your diary entries said as much:
September 1st. Unspeakable closeness
and then drenching, tepid rain. Leon
silent. Birds crashing through the canopy,

their colours fabulous, shocking.
I look forward to your book,
the launch, the crush, the dry
empty feeling once it's finished.

Needs Must

I heard him from the other room,
apologising. He was saying, 'Baby,
even Moses got excited
when he saw the promised land.'

If I wasn't so preoccupied
I'd chuckle. As it is I'm writing this poem
and to make sure I get in a rhyme
for Marie Antoinette

I've made a note of it. Likewise
the part where I compare adolescence
to a dull essence. My work for today?
How to be a Difficult Poet without Boring You.

I intend to go right to the edge of the map
but not fall off, to be beguiling
in an awkward way, like a pretty girl
with a cough. Will that be OK?

Downstairs, in Conference Suite B,
someone is explaining he's conscious of time
so he's going to be brief.
I think I should ignore that.

I think you should too
because I needs must mention the girl again.
She's sitting up in bed now with nothing on
her mind, watching TV and weeping.

How Copenhagen Ended

1.

How Copenhagen began:
nomadic hunters followed the lichen-
and moss-eating reindeer
into post-glacial Denmark.
Eventually the reindeer lit-out
for yet more northern territories,
but those stone-age Danes
dug-in, sowing seeds in the ash
of their slash and burn,
living cheek by jowl with stock
through impossible winters
and interring their ancestors vertically.

2.

The Little Mermaid
sweats and weeps
her way through drizzly afternoons

while tourists gape
disappointedly at her
smooth, childlike nudity,

or, in the orderly Scandinavian silence
of triple-glazed viewing galleries,
watch locked ice loosen

into the edgy, faceted surface
of the Baltic and gulls
upended in water

like lumps of snow,
sipping extortionate coffee.

3.

This is the toothpick
Gorm the Old used
to winkle-out bits
of fermenting herring
from his unspeakable teeth.

Here we have a fine example
of the language
of pornography:
a man swallowing
his own tongue.

This appears to be a silver septum.
Cnut has left us
a signature, and Sweyn
a small ornamental clasp
of some sort.

Rubble fetched up
by freak tides some say is masonry
from great building work,
others that it is no less
than evidence, sentimental mementoes

of that mythical land,
America.

The Hop

(New Poems 2006)

Part One

Reading and Light and Her

Reading and Light and Her

She is unaware of what the light is
doing, how it is resounding
in the coil of her earring, how it floats
around those wisps of hair that invite us

to consider the back of her neck
more closely, especially the critical point
where her pearls fasten
and the cold spill of lit air begins to break

onto her shoulder-blade. She just goes
on reading, staring at the inset
illustration, figuring it all out. Impelled
by a restless physics, light grazes

the side of her face. Words pass
between the page and her, and then through
her, everything washed in light, saying
what light is, our best guess.

The Hop
(or Whatever Happened to Gladys Allen's Fancy?)

Remember when we used to shake a leg
to The Missing Duck or The Rufty Tufty,
The Little Tickle or The Toy Giraffe?
We were quite the item under candy-coloured lights.
Incautiously exceeding stated doses,
we would cut a rug to The Chinese Breakdown,
The Loch Ness Monster, The Silly Threesome
and The Baldyquash. Who would've thought
there'd come a time when hardly anyone knew
how to do The Daft Willy or The Physical Snob?
Now all you get are funny looks
if you ask a girl if she'd like to Double Hot Fudge
or Fivepenny Bit. There's no way
you'd ever catch anyone under eighty
Stripping the Willow or Buttering
the Horse's Ear. What we've lost
is what it takes to do The Emptied Bladder,
The Slippery Swing, The Maid Peeped Out
or The Demented Seagull. Between the wars
we'd famously strut our slightly less than funky stuff
to the horribly prophetic Between the Wars,
when the fiendishly difficult Barbarini's Tambourine
was the saviour of the orthopaedic corset trade.
Many's the lass went limping back
down unlit lanes after trying just that
bit too hard to master The Return
of the Antelope or The Wibsey Squib.
While The Haggis Thrash and The Tumbling Tom
would pack A&E most Friday nights.
Don't get me started on The Moral Slop.
Didn't I hear somebody say
we were due a revival of The Dainty Duncan -
which we used to know as The British Sorrow?
Whatever happened to Gladys Allen's Fancy,
The Weaver's Gallopede and The Old Aw Shucks?
And what's that thing they do today?
The Shapes in Church or The Vomiting Dog?
Well I've seen it and it's laughable.

Wood Asks

A response to the photograph 'Early Morning, January,
Commonhill Wood No. 4 , The Chilterns, 2004' by Robert Davies

Do you remember being in this forest
when air was the colour of tracing paper

and trees were brushed on a wash of mist
like x-rayed bones, like a diagram

of the lung? Do you remember deeper
in the catalogue of branches how the sky began

to teem then drip with light? Do you
remember the scuffle and mush of litter

underneath your boots, the soft give of rot,
the crack and crush of greenish stuff?

Do you remember roots reaching into the dark
chest of the earth for something, and what

that was was the silence of air and light
that became the sound of your listening?

Do you remember being in this forest
and what it was you were doing there?

The Sunday Afternoons

Here they come, the Sunday Afternoons,
looming over the landscape like great wings.
God is abroad and has left His calling card,
so we huddle indoors watching the Battle of the Atlantic
being fought for us one more time in black and white.

This is the era of going next door to use
the phone, the age of half-day closing, an epoch
chroniclers feel could be more than adequately covered
by a footnote. Everyone has an older brother to look up to,
with a job he despises and a fiancé called Maxine

to drag him round the shops on Saturday mornings,
who threatens violence if you go near his aftershave.
But for now we are sitting peaceably in the front room,
thinking that later it might fair up and reflecting
by then it won't matter anyway. The Sunday Afternoons,

replete with bathos and ennui - if anyone could be bothered
to find the dictionary and look up what that means -
given over to regrets and essays about the Corn Laws,
which are often one and the same thing. The whole kit and caboodle
feeling like metaphysical indigestion.

That increment of history where dreams were stalled;
where washing was folded and stacked in airing cupboards;
where celebrity ebbed-out its half-life in reported speech;
the point in the planet's rotation requiring someone
to coin the term 'Hancockian'; the lie of potential ...

They are still here in a world that no longer smells of gravy,
that accounts sushi and pizza almost passé, where television
is exponentially various but essentially wallpaper,
and someone from the sacred past is reading or having a bath,
or both. While the Sunday Afternoons, like gods on horseback,

are thundering down a sky the colour of scrubbed pans,
in an ectoplasmic flicker of bluish light,
weighting the seconds, the minutes, the hours, the days,
with a patented mix of boredom and duty they call
Real Time. They pass no comment. They simply look on.

Chameleon

To step on to a rock and slowly become
the surface of that rock, its smooth brownness,
its interstitial spatter of moss.

To stare out
from ball-turret eyes
at the world you have become.

To find yourself so delicately
adjusted to the truth of objects
that you blush at their sudden reality.

To feel yourself colour to the roots
of your exquisitely coiled tail
at the touch of another.

To become the screen
on which the world shows
the film of itself to itself.

To be well-known for camouflage,
to be singled-out for fitting-in.
To never know each evening

whose skin you'll wake up in.

At the Horological Institute

They are what they seem,
it's just that there are so many of them
here. The superior, the rare,
the unfamiliar. This one's straight out of Dickens,

painted face and gilded decoration,
loitering in the withdrawing room
like the shade of an old cigar.
Whole boxes full of nothing but dull motion.

Here's a beauty went all the way to the moon and back,
spooky as one of Einstein's twins.
They call out at intervals, sing
boring little songs we never tire of.

A Hill in Lincolnshire

A long way to walk
just to stand
looking out

on the fields;
numberless
ridges and hedges

furred in places
by a blur of blossom;
parishes and villages.

The sky,
empty today
but for a few stray

clouds, buzzes
with ghost-squadrons coming
and going from the aerodrome

reverted at last
to beets and potatoes.
I look down

on the spire of St. John's.
And how do I know?
A mile ago

an old man told me.
Baptised
and married there

once
upon at time,
was what he said.

The Galloway Field at Ashington Colliery
for Oliver Kilbourn

There are twenty-eight ponies in the Galloway Field,
the colliery heaped-up behind them. Smoke
from the chimneys bleeds yellow and grey
into a sliced-bread and dishwater sky.

What light it lets through falls on the backs of the ponies
as they bend to pasture, then canter a little
with tails streaming out, or stand
companionably facing each other.

Beneath them the great inverted cathedral
extends for miles its prop-bolstered aisles
and occasional side-chapels where a man might unbuckle
his spine if he wasn't too tall.

In the innocent air with the world at their feet
are twenty-eight ponies waiting to slip
into harness and darkness where something like childhood
will leave them. For now

they know only the light
and the cool of the morning, the clouds
and a breeze from the east, the wet grass,
the simple affection of men passing by.

Epigrammatic
after Martial

Happiness? A steady income
from a steady job; an agreeable hearth;
no correspondence with solicitors;
not too much work in town; a chilled
mind in a well-filled body; old saws
and cherished friends; a healthy appetite;
good, plain food; quiet evenings;
a loyal partner with a sense of adventure;
sufficient sleep but not too much;
acceptance of whatever's yours;
side-stepping sarcasm and power-games;
no fear of the end and no desire for it.

The Future Body

The future body floats
in its own decline. Not smoothed-
      out like a sheet, but overrun
      by time, fissured, sunken, worn

thin, almost luminous. The way
the light wears in you barely
      feel it, until you are practically nothing
      but a glove of light. Skin flakes, eyelashes

splinter, hair sails on the breeze;
decay grinds cells
      into a sort of fragrance. Somehow
      at one with cathedrals, the body

powders to nothing. Stripped
of its vital energies it becomes cloth,
      has weight like bolts of silk have
      weight. Thoughts become colours, wavelengths

skimming air. The future body sheds
its fear, is body entirely,
      all corporeality and shadows.
      Earthiness takes over, its yearning

to become and then consume itself
in earth. It welcomes dirt,
      breathes corruption, has no use
      for niceties, apologies,

we are no longer to be so
impressed by its subtle gifts,
      its pleasures … item: to lie
      in the bath in the evening

listening to birdsong as it clamours
through a cracked top-light, or
      item: watching steam escape, its gauze
      unstitch itself, or

item: the impeccably palpable ear lobe
of a loved one, or … As light
      sifts lazily through frosted glass,
      deepening by degrees from palest blue

to indigo, the body eases from all this,
like a liner setting out
                on some luxurious voyage,
                the only sound

coming from the upper deck is the crack of ice,
in cocktails, maybe, the slow dissolve
                of elements in elements.
                The future body unlocks

chained-up codes, in strings they spill,
unravelling into the immaterial.
                It interrupts itself in mid embrace
                and falls away, a heap of clothes

collapsed onto a chair, a pile of wires
pulled out from a wall, the signals gone
                somewhere else or routed back
                into themselves to clot,

like solder. That's why rivers flood
or parch to scars, why snakes
                shed paper cases, to escape
                the future body, why trees

open their palms and beg whoever
haunts the sky. It makes no odds.
                The future body is itself a seed
                within a seed. All you can do

is hold on tight to what you are:
the vellum of your skin,
                its watermarks, its secret
                marginalia, rip cords

of muscle, the impossible
hydraulics of the soul, until
                the future body is alone
                at last inside its flesh and bone.

Misplaced Prologue

Isolation is one way of knowing yourself
too well. Reality is a big confusion about beliefs.
Either that or it's literal and numb.

The Industrial Revolution exiled God
and went headlong for steam engines and bottled scotch.
The Romantic poets saw a gap in the market for landscapes

and moody weather. They left us their unfinished project,
strange, metaphorical animals and sentimental pity.
Forgetting weighs nothing. Horses the colour of violins

graze in a field on the edge of a wilderness
known locally as Takla Makan (which approximates as:
you'll get in but you'll never get out). It takes time to waste time.

It can often take longer. Photography is mysterious.
People being photographed very rarely know what to do with their hands.
Reality is alienating politics and so

the alienating, sophisticated playfulness
of modern poetry can sometimes almost make sense.
Unlike the moon which nothing more than a ball

of flaking plaster someone forgot to sweep up.
After the flood the sky pulled its hatches open.
Light fell like rain upon the tongue.

Part Two

Sailing Alone Around the World

Sailing Alone Around the World

I kept breaking down
but then a few words would filter in
over the transom and transform me.

It was a question
of language, I mean
it being equal to the problem.

Take, for example, that prince among pronouns,
the simple downstroke.
Squeezed behind it, the labyrinth of identity.

I broke down again yesterday.

There's something about flowing
and fixedness and how completion's
an impossibility, worse than that,
a bizarre and inconceivable conceit.

So I pulled myself up
on this rickety, bourgeois artefact.

The sky all flinty and chipped,
like a chipped china owl, I thought to myself,
or a late photograph of Virginia Woolf
not long before she waded into the weedy Ouse.

Crowds wave giddily from distant quays,
afflicted by a pitiless mania
for ends and beginnings.

But the part of me the sea first spoke to
is sleeping now, and the breeze
is a clean lance on which I fasten my favour.

There are no really good rhymes for fo'c'sle,
so I won't get hung up about that either.

Enough I should wallow
in this powdery, veiled light
which I swallow like milled jade.

Heroes

Not one for literature or life, I read
comics, *Captain America*, *The Incredible Hulk*,
The Fantastic Five; second-hand,
imported glamour flickering on market stalls
in the 1960s. The air was full of rumours.

Were the Beatles smoking dope? Had the Maharishi
thing gone too far? And something about Aden
or Adenauer. Clearly the world
would need saving. And pretty soon.
Fish-counters gleamed with wet light,

scallop shells fluted and white
as the marble columns of classical Athens;
the hissing of coffee bars; meat on hooks;
shag-pile pillared shrines of carpet remnants;
roots and leaves still clinging to the earth.

I wandered down to the bus station, lost
in twisting crowds, caught up in yarns
spun about Spiderman and his sickly aunt.
Webs and lines, Thor's hammer,
The Human Torch, The Thing ...

I opened the kitchen door
on a room full of clouds. Olympus,
West Yorkshire. My mother stewing sheets.
'Home is the hero,' she smiled.
'Go quietly, your father's asleep.'

Autobiographical Stanzas

I lopped-off the beginning
and the end of it,
leaving only the central part,

and called this my life.
On cold mornings
when I was growing up

sometimes the fire wouldn't light
until we showed it
yesterday's headlines.

At 43 I decided
I was too old
for training shoes, and so

was unable to write
the poem 'Man Running
Away From Himself'. Something

I had been planning
for a while. Had I
anything to confess, I would

have become a confessional poet.
Alas, viewed from
a comfortable reading distance

my life is so ordinary
it disappears. Consequently
I am not a poet. Perhaps

this is what makes me interesting.

Bicycles Round a Tree in West Yorkshire
(with due acknowledgement to Ruth Padel and Andy Goldsworthy)

We're talking different kinds of class-distinction here.
Melvin Dawson's bike was his dad's bike,
which was in turn his dad's elder brother's.

Consequently it weighs about the same as a Morris Minor
and has a tubular metal framework
welded in front of the handlebars,

where a large basket might be accommodated.
David Brook's model, on the other hand, is factory-fresh.
Metallic blue, embedded with glittery filaments

like the sparkles on a Ludwig drum kit,
it has a sprung seat in cream vinyl
with matching panniers and mudguards,

and is light enough to lift over a low wall
with one hand. For myself, this season
I am riding a brown, three-year old Raleigh

with the by-now un-vogueish smaller wheels.
It does, however, sport an impressive twist-grip gear-change
and amber diamond-cut reflectors set into the pedals.

We are idling away the afternoon in the straggly shade
of a small stand of apple trees. Around us and in every direction
rhubarb stretches as far as the eye can see.

Melvin is lately returned from Sunday School
and hands round for our inspection a bookmark
printed with the names of the nine choirs of angels:

Seraphim, Cherubim, Thrones, Dominions,
Virtues, Powers, Princedoms, Archangels
(which he pronounces *arch*-angels, as in *arch*-villains)

and *Angels*. The three of us stare up at splintered bits of sky
between the apple-boughs, ostensibly but only vaguely
contemplating the social hierarchy of heaven.

After a while we pick up our bikes
and, manoeuvring them over the bumpy verge,
strike out up the hill where, for some reason,

a superabundance of gravity seems to have collected.
We travel up the slope in almost slow-motion,
like men wading through quicksand.

At the top we look down on an earthly paradise of rhubarb
then peel-off to our own villages, what farewells we have
blowing back and away over our innocent shoulders.

Roofspace

When the cowboy builders moved out
my father stuck his head through the trapdoor
into the roofspace

and surveyed the small devastation
of rubble: jumbled, calcified extrusions
of mortar, fillets of cement,

smashed laths and fragmentary roof tiles.
A lunar landscape
only inches above the bedrooms.

Once he'd finished swearing
revenge we shinned-up there with shovels -
fearful of the frail ceiling plaster -

gingerly, to dig out the detritus.
As we lowered down percussive sackfuls,
the soft-core loads gave off a muted chime,

a dampened *dinging* sound,
the lumpy, grey waste
grating against itself.

We dumped it in the garden
in an uneven heap,
like the mad replica mountain

Richard Dreyfus makes and remakes in *Close Encounters*,
then squeezed almost weightless,
outsize rolls of fibreglass insulation

into the space. Each one unfurled
noiselessly, wadding
the emptiness, quilting the atmosphere

with a special quality -
a thick, rich nothingness,
almost the inverse of sound.

Our skin was prickly for days
with microscopic filaments of fibreglass
we couldn't forget,

like knowledge of that silence,
or the flutter of dust
in the fragile wedge of scooped-out air

that kept the sky from falling in.

A Picture
for Fionna Murray

I have spent the last few days
working on this picture
for you. In it there is a tree,
a yellow chair (the sort
with a straight back and a cane
seat), a sky the colour of lilacs
and, on the chair, a bundle
of grey twigs. I hope
you like it. I hope you can see
your hand in it. The tree is
probably some sort of chestnut,
but I wouldn't know a chestnut
from a beech and I wouldn't know
a beech if it walked up to me
and introduced itself. I don't know
what it means and this is why
I've been working on it: so that
I can send it to you and you can
tell me. Do you think the chair
is you or are you the tree?
Are the twigs and the chair symbols
of resurrection? Is the sky
in any way important?
Is the fact that it is clearly winter
at all relevant? It's not difficult
to see why I needed to get some help
in figuring out what I've done.
I'm sure you will
come through on this for me
and tell me what's behind it,
and if there's anything to praise
in it. After all these years
surely we can speak honestly,
in words we can both understand.

Trouble with the Rat Race

The house is someone else's, the falling
to the floor is mine. It happens
sometimes. I get used to it.

I pointed to a vase of flowers.
I felt it was like me. I can't
say how. I said as much. I wanted

to but couldn't. Ever felt
like that? When I looked through the window
bits of blue were pasted in

the heavens' otherwise glum light.
'Is there a secret to all this?' I asked
as she lay down beside me.

We stared up at the sky's immense
archives. It looked just like a sketch
in ink. I hauled myself up

like an anchor. 'Trouble with
the rat race is,' she said, 'that even if
you win you're still a rat.'

Praises of the Hare

As I roved out among the lanes and hedgerows
I came upon a face regarding mine,
a small, leaf-coloured face among the leaves.
Soon enough he showed himself: the stook-deer,
the skipper, stubble-stag of the soft suede horn.

We stood there - both of us doused in light,
composed, it seemed, of so much light - not knowing
what to say or do. And so we took
the lesser part and quietly remained,
like an allegory or a weathervane.

Much pressing business elsewhere, after a while
he abruptly turned and left and I roved back
to the car where it was hot. Shortly the rain fell.
It had not been falling but now it fell decisively
over fields and ditches. I opened my little book.

I meant to write down how it is the man
the hare has met will never have the better of it
lest he speak the praises of the hare.
Vainly I rummaged in the glove compartment.
My friend had gone and now I had no pen.

My friend had gone into the world of rain.
I watched leaves flickering like compass needles.
I trawled the lint out of my jacket pockets.
I waited in the unimportant rain.
Until it stops, I thought, I will stay here.

Memory

Of all of us I was the one who went
to the four corners of language but
I don't take any pride in that.

I did it, I think, by accident
because it was the closest I came to something
to believe in, although I have always believed

in music and, much later, painting, and that,
I think, because of the quiet of galleries and the people
I met who said yes to looking and thinking

about looking, like my friend
from years ago, we wrote to each other,
but lately not for a while. In one of her letters

she said *what do we care, we have*
the universe – no we haven't,
that was a lie, and once we lay on the floor

together and that was okay,
we had important things to discuss.
When she left I fed memory with a plate of bones.

Part Three

Poetry is Your Friend

Poetry is Your Friend

It's undeniably true, life
weathers you. There's no doubt
about that. Gardens crammed
with slightly creepy little elves,
a van parked on a deserted lane,
the sky almost purple when you look out.

That's when you turn to poetry.
You may not know it of course,
but that's what you'll be doing.
You're doing it right now, superficially
despite yourself, riding this wave
of energy out of nowhere. It feels good,

doesn't it? Like a high-sugar drink
or that special moment, you know
the one. It's here to help
even if it sometimes forgets,
gets all wrapped up
in counting syllables and such.

It wants you like a tyrant or the sun.

Advice from Parnassus

Literature is a fine career for a young person.
It's so straightforward. You just write
down your deepest feelings. In fact
they don't even have to be deep, any feelings
will do. The media can't get enough.
Everyone knows this.
If you want to you can describe mountains
or sex scenes, what people say, the way
they stare into each other's eyes
as if desperately trying to decode secret messages.

There's so much scope. You slide your coin
in the slot, take a swing at the horizon
and see what comes up. It's a breeze.
Don't waste your time on cybernetics,
the greasy corporate pole. That sort of thing
is strictly for numps and loobies. Drop by
any time, and remember, when you enter a room
carry yourself magnificently, especially your head,
which you should think of as a vase of lilacs,
preferably painted by Chardin.

'Poems of Universal Wisdom & Beauty'

I forgive everyone. I'm like
that. I don't gossip too much.
I'm a kind of hero. The moon
is like a big empty plate up there,
don't you think? No? Okay.
I'm a very democratic writer.

Most days I'm at work on my magnum opus:
'Poems of Universal Wisdom & Beauty'.
I'm understandably excited. Music drifts
through from the other room
like smoke while I type away
merrily. When lunch arrives I eat it.

I'm trying to free myself
from the idea that intelligence can only be
conveyed by thought, especially
the complex, allusive sort. Readability
is my new thing. Readability
equals intelligence.

Sonnet About a Handgun with Diamonds

I am writing this sonnet about
a handgun with diamonds. The light
fires off the facets and dazzles.
But this is a handgun alright.

We are swinging through somewhere quite louche
in a taxi that smells of incense.
The mirror is hung with red tassels.
The driver is black and farouche.

If none of this makes any sense,
remember this sonnet's about
a handgun encrusted with jewels

and, as such, the usual rules
should be left at the door. Got that? Right.
A handgun is what this is about.

A Postcard to Martin Stannard

I'm writing regarding my head. Do you think anything can be done about it? You can tell me. I can take it. Birdsong occurs frequently in my poetry (here it is again). I mean, I know it's preferable to stars, but not how preferable. And what about horses? Because I know horses stand for common sense. Where do you stand on the whole 'building a bridge between you and the reader' issue? When should I bring in the horses?

The Duck's Back and How it Got Like That

You have taken to returning
to the old notebooks,
where the other life is,
'the properly narrated one',
where you consider the duck's back
and how it got like that,
the morphology of clouds,
how stars explode, the habits
of gravity and time. These days
you wake up in the dark

and ask yourself what you know:
the names of the Telemark saboteurs;
how the best way of writing about it
is never writing about it; that the light
at the end of the tunnel is no chink
in the gloved and greaved murk
of Erebus, neither is it the apocryphal
oncoming locomotive. It is only
some bastard with a torch.
He is not looking for you.

The News and The Weather

Too much has already been said

about the spring. More than enough
ink has been squandered on the fall.

It would be impossible to entirely cast out
the volumes that dwell on light.
That winter is marching steadily

down from the hills is as much
yesterday's news as ripples of sand
on the beach being like something
or something else. The wet-linen

colour of almost every cloud
in literature is, frankly, boring.
It is time to address other things:
empty boxes of rain that are sometimes
trees, the neglected battalions of grass …

Just a Few Questions from the Panel

Why do you want to be a poet?
What sort of work do poets do?
What, in your view, is the difference

between the work of a poet
and the work of a civil engineer?
What would you say

if you were asked to write concrete poetry?
What would you say
if you were asked to build a concrete boat?

Why do some poems rhyme?
What makes a slum?
What is a Found Poem

and where might you find one?
What is conservative dentistry? What should be done
in the case of an elderly person who steals a bar of soap?

What are the qualities of a sound net-ball defence?
Why do you want to be a poet?
Is there a future in fish farming?

Part Four

The End of Side One

The End of Side One

It rarely happens these digital days,
that skating away
into coughs and crackles
> which meant you had to lumber across
> and flip the disc
> on that soft pad of flesh
> at the base of your fingers.
Sometimes, if the light was right,
it was almost petrol-shimmery,
like a crow's wing,
and banded like a target
or a treestump.

This interruption, then, the getting up
or sitting there listening
to the amplifier's dull hum,
its impedance -
> measured in ohms
> and designated by the symbol Ù ,
> which means the end of the beginning,
> or at least the place where things begin again -
wasn't this boring,
domestic discontinuity
a bit like finding yourself
in the middle of things,
suddenly awake to the world,
the daynoise and birdsong
floating like motes
on the surface of silence?

Or maybe it was somehow more
like the dream of a better life,
one swept clean
> of all that sticky drek,
> the fluff and lint,
> rid at last of those clicks and cracks,
> those potholes in the road
> going nowhere.
And sometimes isn't there still
the sense of needing
to pull up in between acts,
draw breath,
say *That's enough of that,*
and start over?

Sonny Rollins on the Williamsburg Bridge

In the middle of the dark wood
of his life a man might decide
that a change of direction is what's required,

and take to going out nights
onto the Williamsburg Bridge where Manhattan's lights
are a glittery sheen that skates

on the East River -
and sit among the noise and glare
playing the saxophone for whoever.

He blows variations
on St. Thomas, Body & Soul, but no-one really listens,
except maybe the Brooklyn trains

that shuffle in four,
ferrying souls over the dark water,
a back-beat to the singular encounter

of breath and air,
which anyone there
would tell you is a person's only true career.

'So What'
(the Miles Davis group, 1959)

A kind of falling away;
a phrase as clear as a photographic negative
held to the light then replaced on the relative
obscurity of the tabletop. A stray

beat trapped on dimpled snare-skin
with a fly-swat snap.
Miles is on top
floating notes on the thinnest of thin

air. Who cares that one of the tape machines
is running a semitone slow? Not me,
I'm still in the milky haze

of the crib, soaking up my father's besotted gaze
when Coltrane's
solo starts to set everything free.

Hank Williams' Last Highway

          The drive should've taken him
through wintry Virginia
                    and Kentucky, as it was
          it stopped short,
200 miles
     outside Knoxville, Tennessee

                    where a ragged state-line
traces the scars of colonial wars,

          the mazey chain of the Appalachians.

That New Year's morning he lay in the back of the car,

                    hat pulled low, a whisky bottle
          wedged in his crotch.
                    A few cold stars glittered
through panicky, orbital ambulance lights.

In Canton, Ohio the promoter's phone
          ringing off the hook.

Hutton's Unconformity

'The mind seemed to grow giddy from looking so far
into the abyss of time'

James Hutton, geologist (1726 - 1796)

Buttoned into his coat
the way a man is buttoned
into his own century,
Hutton was facing up to a gale
that was blowing right out of history,
all the way from Norway, maybe.

The vertical ridges and horizontal planes
meant something to him
although he had no names for them.
Strange for him to be the only man
on earth who knew time
had its unconformities, corners

around which one might peek
and stare down a long avenue
leading back to the present moment.
The unfathomable North Sea shattered
over basalt crags, sending smithereens
of spume in all directions.

It was bitterly cold as Hutton sketched
the grooved and fluted surfaces.
His hands were numb. His gaze
grew dizzy at the cliffs' unstable edges.
He thought he saw the past
like a pile of books,

or angel cake, each layer
coloured and distinct, permeated
with its own essence; pale ages
suffused with the pigment of petals,
millennia stained by the bodies
of countless crushed beetles.

Vermeer

The sun shines on a little patch of yellow wall and the sky is a monument to Holland, bruised and golden, pewter and best plate. A land of cloudbanks and damp cattle, lanes lost to hedgerows and rain. In drawing-rooms lace-collared girls pick out Spanish tunes on small guitars, or stand in long skirts at virginals attempting some of the simpler airs of William Byrd. A housemaid snores, mice chase about her feet, while a whey-faced young woman holds up a letter to winter light high windows grudgingly admit. Split seconds trapped in sticky oils, like flies in amber sap, give off the unmistakable vibrations of presence; how life, though cross-connected, sings in each thing separately, is sadder and more beautiful for that. A city gate reflected in a river, the rotting hull of an old barge, some milk falling forever in a white thread, light unexpectedly finding a pearl earring as eternally she turns her head.

A Guided Tour of the Air Museum

Here is the yellow air of London
in the nineteenth century, smelling
of gin and orphans and axle-grease.
Over there is the bright blue air of Umbria
in the 1550s, loud with the thrap of pennants,
the clatter of lances.
And this is night air from beneath
the Brooklyn Bridge, grazed
with the silence of Hart Crane.
That row of jars contains the air
from several Georgian withdrawing rooms,
mostly exhaled in secret sighs
of lust and longing. Musky and dotted
with flies is the air that hung close
to the days and raiment of John the Baptist,
while the air Vermeer painted is clear
as light after a shower of rain
one otherwise flawless September morning.
Remarkably alike are the little boost of air
that ruffled Napoleon's kiss-curl
at Waterloo and the final E flat
from the euphonium on the Titanic.
Fixed between two smoky plates of glass
is an oily ghost that hovered
for decades over a pre-war tin of Swarfega.
The faint opacity of the vitrine
on your left is the *Yes* of a girl from 1904.
That concludes our tour.
Be careful as you leave
not to inhale the gift shop.
Just my little joke, ladies and gentlemen.
Please, remember your guide.

The Clown's Resignation Letter

It appears there are only so many
ways a man can make a fool
of himself before the penny
drops. When they move the stool

as he doltishly goes to sit down
for the zillionth time - he gets it.
He chose to become a clown,
but now, well, he regrets it.

The pie-in-the-face that seemed
such an art is simply an insult
added to injury. Themed
humiliation - the slick result

of endless, refining rehearsals -
drenches him in despair,
induces sad reversals
of ambition. Orange hair

sprouting from the bald-cap,
once satiric, is now ironic.
The all-consuming cold slap
of a codfish dull and chronic

as the progress of arthritis
through outsize, flapping feet
that in earlier days were as light as
a ballerina's. Defeat

may be comic, but it is defeating
all the same. If anyone knows
about timing, I should. Life is fleeting.
I am enclosing the nose.

Study for 'Francis Bacon (Drunk)'

Someone is asking, in French,
if he believes in God.

Non. Il n'existe pas.
So what does he believe in?

Beauty. The beauty of men.
He's rolling around, he can barely remain

upright. He's keeping on
the move to keep from falling

over. He has a glass in his hand.
(How many times have you seen him

without a glass in his hand?)
Does he go to galleries to look

at great paintings? Not much. No.
Well, he goes but he doesn't

spend long. He'll just stand
in front of a Rembrandt, say,

for a few moments then come away
with a violently

invigorated connection to life.
What's that hard light

in his eyes, concise
as a diamond? Shall we

open another bottle? Of course
we'll open another bottle. Now,

he fucking well hopes so, but
has everyone got what they want?

Love on a Farm Boy's Wages

I have fought my way through the hedge
for you. I have stolen flowers.
I am probably standing too close.

I have come to ask you out.
So will you come out with me?
We could walk along the hedgerows.

We could try and keep in step.
We could just see what it feels like.
We could talk about whatever you wanted.

We could catch the bus to the next village.
We could agree there is virtually nothing
to do in a dump like this.

After all, you and I are alike.
We are similarly alienated.
We are both unsure quite what that means.

We would both like Sky Digital.
So will you come out with me?
I've ruined my good shoes to ask you.

That must mean something to a girl
like you. I know a lot about sheep.
There is a great deal more to know.

The Victorians

Their hats, their telephones
like candlesticks, their fear
of piano-legs, their aspidistras
were some of the biggest
in the world, their harking back
to days of chivalry, their coats
of arms, their love of black,
their historically remarkable vocabulary,
their rules, their ruling
half the globe, their love affairs
with stags, limp pheasants, doe-
eyed orphans, ornaments and fringes,
their inventions and their devastatingly,
immaculately engineered
constructions, their first, their second
and third class compartments,
their footmen, butlers, pastry cooks,
their under parlour-maids, their gardeners,
gardeners' boys, their getting lost
in India and Africa, their vast reserves
of industry, their shirtfronts and their lack
of proper contraception, their diseases,
laundered handkerchiefs, their fear of women,
their women's fear, their children
with building bricks and hoops
and sticks, their penny farthings, poverty
and lighter-men, their inky rivers, ink,
pen-wipers, stylographs, their brute
technology of writing, their illiteracy,
their theatre, sense of fun, their love of hardwoods,
corsetry, long underwear, umbrellas,
bombazine, their need to cover up
as much as possible, yea unto
the brink of complete asphyxiation,
their dragging dresses making hissing
noises, no-one saying anything
because the risk of saying something
out of place was almost lethal,
their noisy clocks that needed winding
with a key, their string quartets,
their mines, their echoing asylums, slums,
gin palaces and churches, their factories
that looked like churches milling souls

into the raw material of empire,
their dreams, their miseries, their heartaches,
operettas, melodramas, their wallpaper,
their penny-dreadfuls, shilling shockers,
epic poems, hobbies, butterfly collections,
sick perversions, boot-blacks, hymn-books,
sweat-stains, shameful thoughts and actions,
their tea-sets, jeweled cigar-cutters, day-
excursions, scepticism, radical philosophies,
their lockets, portrait miniatures, lump sugar, things
in gelatine, their gradual decline, their putty,
brass and paint, their quite spectacular
but ultimately doomed moustaches.

Previous Collections by CJ Allen:

The Art of Being Late for Work, (Amazing Collossal Press, 1994)
Elfshot, (Waldean Press, 1997)
How Copenhagen Ended, (Leafe Press, 2003)

Acknowledgements:

Thanks are due to the editors who have published these poems before – in
books and magazines.

Several of the poems included in 'The Hop' were awarded prizes in competi-
tions, namely:

Chameleon – Lancaster LitFest Poetry Competiton 2000
Roofspace – Yorkshire Open Poetry Competition 2000
At the Horological Institute – Leicester Open Poetry Competition 2000
Sailing Alone Around the World, Sonnet About a Handgun with Diamonds,
Sonny Rollins on the Williamsburg Bridge – Nottingham Open Poetry Compe-
tition 2003
Bicycles Round a Tree in West Yorkshire – Lancaster LitFest Poetry
Competition 2003
Heroes, Hank Williams' Last highway – Ver Poets Open Poetry competition
2004
Love on a Farm Boy's Wages – Newark Open Poetry Competition 2004
Wood Asks - Djanogly Gallery Landscape Photography Poetry Competition
2004
'So What' – Ver Poets Open Poetry Competition 2005
The Sunday Afternoons – Nottingham Open Poetry Competition 2005
The Victorians – Yorkshire Open Poetry Competition 2005
The Galloway Field at Ashington Colliery, The Clown's Resignation Letter –
Ilkley Literature Festival Poetry Competition 2005
Reading and Light and Her, Praises of the Hare – Lancatser LitFest Poetry
Competition 2005
Just a few Questions from the Panel – Newark Open poetry Competition 2005

Lightning Source UK Ltd.
Milton Keynes UK
27 November 2009

146768UK00001B/184/A